A VIEW FROM GRIEF'S WINDOW

*Ten Lessons I Learned From
the Death of My Parents*

BY NEIL GILLILAND, PH.D.

Contents

This book is dedicated to my brothers and their wives who cared for dad and mom (especially mom in the last years of her life). Blaine and Beverly would take mom to their home in Indiana for several weeks each summer and loved and cared for her. Mike and Tami picked up mom most Saturdays and loved on her all day. And most of all to Frank and Corina who kept mom in their home for nearly nine years. I am deeply indebted to my family.

Introduction

Before I begin to walk you through the landscape of lessons I learned from the death of my parents, I want to give you a look into their lives (at least from my perspective). For many years, I wanted to honor my mom and dad because they had done so much for me. I decided I would write tributes to them and send them to their local newspaper without telling them. I wrote dad's first and then several years later I wrote mom's. Much to my joy the newspaper printed them. Here they are.

A Hero for All Seasons

Slocum Station, the little community that wraps itself around the bends of Ward's Run seems a rather unlikely place for the making of heroes. But real heroes aren't made; somehow, they just become. Unless you have been dubbed with some extraordinary ability in athletics or the arts, or won single-handedly a great battle, the odds of attaining hero status are at best, slim. And to be quite honest, my hero is and never was any of those things. By the time he was three or four, he, along with a sister, were orphaned. He has lived the next 90+ years in Slocum Station. So, if one were in search of the type of adventures that are required to produce true heroes, I really don't imagine you would choose Slocum. But maybe, just maybe, true heroes are more than what they do; it's who they are. You see my hero does not wear an armor that shines with brilliance, or never accomplished some daring feat in some distant land. He is just a dad...my dad.

As the dogwoods begin to bloom each spring around my Tennessee home, I know what is taking place in Slocum. The robins will be following close behind Dad as they gather earthworms while he turns the soil in his garden for another season of planting. I often wonder why the President doesn't assign Dad to the task force to combat world hunger. By summer's end he is up half the night worried about who could come and carry away the baskets full of excess vegetables. Taxpayers would take note of his cost cutting. For example, standing in the corner of the shed is Dad's hoe. The metal blade is half gone now. Dad bought that hoe the first year he and Mom were married, and weeds have unsuccessfully ducked that same hoe over the past 67+ years. Not only has he provided fresh vegetables, he has worked. For some 45 years, he made the trip from Slocum to the steel mill. In the early years, he made the trip on foot. Why...because he had a wife and family. The point is this: Dad provided by hard work and frugality. I suppose it would be too much to ask everyone to be that way. But then again not everyone chooses to be a hero and that's the sort of things heroes do.

On misty summer mornings, I can still smell the sweet odor of the outdoors he left in the house after a night of fox hunting. It was a sport he loved. I must admit I've never understood the attraction of sitting up all night listening to dogs bark, and arguing with your fellow hunters about which hound was leading the pack. No gun was ever fired; the hunters only listened to old Dixie or Pretty Boy howl at some fox scampering about the hills, laughing at his pursuers. However, my understanding of the philosophical significance of fox hunting shrinks in the light of the life principles those expeditions taught me. The smell that hovers in my memory, along with the thoughts of eager little boys waiting to see if Dad had eaten all the sweet rolls Mom had sent with his Vienna sausages to get him through the long night of rigorous listening and talking, all serve to remind me of this lesson. There were always sweet rolls left. The principle is not complicated: others come first. Dad is just that way, he always thinks of others first. He would never eat the last bite of anything for fear another member of his family or a guest might want it. Quite simply, my dad clothed himself in the cloak of selflessness. I suppose it would be too much to ask everyone to be that way. But then again, not everyone chooses to be a hero and that's the sort of thing heroes do.

The hills of southern Ohio certainly evoke a feeling of warmth each fall, when the trees produce a cacophony of color and a feeling that all is well in the world. Each time I return to the little gray-shingled house in the heart of Slocum, there is that same sense of warmth and security. It wasn't one of those houses where room and rooms were plentiful. You could put the key in the front door and nearly knock out the back window. Yet, despite the lack of space our home was filled with an overwhelming love. Dad loved us. It didn't matter if we accomplished something wonderful that made him swell with pride, or if we disappointed him, he still loved us. But most importantly, Dad loved Mom. I never worried if their marriage would last. I have never even seen them have an argument. Wouldn't our world be a wonderful place if everyone loved their children and their wives the way Dad does? But then again not everyone chooses to be a hero and that's the sort of thing heroes do.

I really don't like winter. Apart from a few days when the world outside dresses itself in bridal white, it's a rather bleak time. I think it is an all too clear reminder of the bleakness of life. Life, far too frequently, seems like a string of one sadness followed by another. My dad's faith in God has provided a constant source of strength when the winds of life blew harder than I thought I could stand. Locked in my memory is the look of sadness I saw on Mom and Dad's faces as my young bride and I returned to Slocum to say goodbye just before leaving to become missionaries in Africa. I knew what he was thinking: "I'll never see my baby boy again." But his faith in the Lord penetrated his tear filled eyes and I knew all would be well. I wonder what life would be like if everyone had Dad's faith and strength? But then again not everyone chooses to be a hero and that's the sort of things heroes do.

The seasons of life have taken their toll on my hero, Ora Gilliland. His once strong body has been spent. It has been a simple yet profound life. Oh, I know he's not perfect and his armor at times has needed polishing and a dab of oil, but his heart hasn't. And, I know that he could not have done it without Mom. I just wish I could repay him, but I can't. I owe too much. The only thing that I can do is to be like him, so one day my little girl can lean over to her playmates, point to me, and say, "That's my daddy, he's my hero."

I love you Dad.

An Angel in an Apron

A few weeks ago, I made the journey once again from my home in Nashville to the rolling hills along the banks of the Ohio River. I still get a bit choked up as I drive around the trip's last curve and see that little gray shingled house in Slocum Station. It's home. I try to make the journey a little more often now, for I know time's cruel hands keep moving on the clock of life. But this trip was different, I realized something that I have had tucked in the back of my mind for a long time, but simply didn't know how to say it.

You see this time, I watched Mom as she did what she has done for 83 years. In the little house, which is so very rich with "home," I listened to the familiar early morning clanging of pans and skillets. My eyes moistened when she asked me the same question she asked every morning, "Do you want me to fix you some regular (milk gravy for you non-Gillilands)." At that moment, as the sun began to peak over the trees on its daily journey across the southern Ohio sky, I realized what my mind had tucked away, some angels wear aprons and I call her Mom.

Mom was not a modern lady. Her bronzed summer skin was not a result of long afternoons basking in the sun next to the pool. This tanned angel's browned skin came from hauling water from the well to the back porch, pouring it into the ringer washer, and hanging the week's laundry on the lines stretched from the big sycamore tree to the coal shed. Her bronzed features were a product of her journeys to brier thickets to pick blackberries or to gather the vegetables growing in the garden to be canned for the long winter months ahead. Her name never appeared on the guest list of fancy restaurants, a trip to town and lunch at the Eighth Street Hamburger Inn or the Towne House in Portsmouth was about as fancy as she got. Chocolate mousse, filet mignon, or shrimp scampi never found their way to her kitchen, but her noodles, "Cowboy" cookies, raisin pie, "regular" and other delights could have only been from the skilled hands of an angel, an angel in an apron.

She has never traveled. She has never seen the sites of the world or even America. Yet she logged thousands of miles. Most of the miles were from Slocum Station to Sciotoville to bring one of us home from ball practice or take us to a game. She wore out several family cars to be in the grandstands, regardless if it was cold and snowy during football season or the blistering heat as her boys of summer took to the baseball field. The distance to the game was of little consequence, the simple truth was she was there. If Frank got a hit or Mike threw a touchdown pass or Blaine sank a free throw, she saw it. While our performance on the athletic field at times wavered, one thing was always consistent and never changed, somewhere in the cheering or jeering crowd sat an angel with eyes filled with a mom's pride. Why? Well, she just loved us and people who love deeply do things like that.

She really loves Dad. In today's world that may seem to be a rather foreign concept. On this trip I watched her, every now and again she would glance at the man she has loved for so many years. You would have thought she was a beautiful young girl, Ruth Yeley, looking into the eyes of her dashing hero, Ora Gilliland. Well the truth is...she was. Oh, I know his dash has slowed to a shuffle, but to her his hero status has gone unchanged. And this aproned angel is still very much in love.

Even more, mom loves God. We never missed church. All my life I have heard her knees crack as she knelt beside her bed every night and prayed. She always prayed out loud. She never knew and I never told her but very often I listened. I listened quietly each night as she asked the Father to watch over her boys and Dad. I heard her pray for our friends and neighbors who were sick or had suffered one of life's alarm moments. Words are far too frail to explain what it did for a teenage boy to hear his mom carry him and place in the lap of Jesus and ask Him to care for her baby boy. When my wife and I were missionaries in Africa, so very often I had this strange sense of peace envelope me. I would look at my watch and I understood. You see, at that moment many miles across the ocean in America, a couple of well-worn knees were popping again. I knew an angel in an apron's son was being carried to the bosom of Jesus.

The gray shingles are faded now on the house where I passed the idyllic days of childhood. The garage that protected our car from the rain, snow, and sun is teetering on the brink of collapse. The cellar door has been replaced and the outhouse at the end of the walkway has been boarded shut. Age has taken a severe toll. Inside the little house the lady who transformed that tiny space into a home has begun to show the same signs that the toll of time takes. She said that when she turned 80 then she would be old. Well if that is true, she has been old for several years now. The smooth skin of the prettiest girl in Slocum has given way to the wrinkles etched into her face by a lifetime of loving, nurturing, and caring for her husband and the four boys who call her Mom. She secured hundreds of band aids on our skinned knees, held cold wash clothes on our heads when we were sick, and greased our chests at bedtime when winter colds knocked. When Mom was there, we knew everything would be okay. I'm 45 years old and still have moments when I wish I could crawl up in her lap and have Mom hold me.

I don't understand a great deal about theology but I do know that my heart will leap with joy if I come around one of the curves of Heaven's roads and see a wee house and as I enter I hear, "Do you want me to fix you some regular?" and I turn and see an angel...an angel in an apron.

I love you Mom.

These tributes laid the foundation for why I knew grief was so very real when their lives were gone. But there have been other griefs that have left their mark and perhaps scars at times. The grief that follows the loss of other loved ones and friends. The intensity of my grief when we left our ministry in Cote d'Ivoire was overwhelming and now more than thirty years later I still feel the pangs. But the lessons I learned about grief from my parents' deaths have given me some new perspectives and hopefully will be an encouragement to you.

— CHAPTER 1 —

The Reality of the View

The view from grief's window is reality
in its harshest form. Grief is real.

Mom was across from me. My brothers and their wives were there. We held hands as we made a circle around dad's bed. It wasn't the bed he had shared with mom for more than 70 years. It was a hospital bed. Hundreds of patients had slept and suffered in that bed. I wish it could have been in their room and their bed; instead it was a nice but non-descript hospital room. There was no feeling of home. There were only tubes, bottles, and whispering noises as we watched him slowly pass from this life. We had watched all morning as each breath was farther apart. And finally, they simply stopped. He was gone. The little old man that had become my hero was dead.

Moments after he took his last breath, my brother, whose hand I held, spoke softly, "Neil can you say a little prayer." I prayed a brief prayer of thanksgiving for the wonderful gift the Father had given our family and then mom kissed the forehead of her beloved who was no longer there. In that moment, with tears making small rivers down my cheeks, I took my first full view from grief's window.

The panorama of dissonant emotions marked their line deep and indelibly across my soul. I felt a sense of peace knowing that dad was now resting in the arms of the Holy One. But at the same moment, as I took my first glimpse from grief's window, the winds of sorrow swept violently across the landscape of my heart. Sorrow's reflection illuminated the room in my inner being whose door had never been opened. But once you have entered into that room you see life differently.

I stood, reluctantly, but with no choice, in the middle of grief's room. We all eventually will stand there. Some stand there many times. It never becomes easier just more familiar. The view from grief's window is painfully real.

Our culture conditions us to avoid grief, to somehow make it less than real. Grief means change. We fight against change because it means what was...is no longer.

We have sanitized death. "He just looks like he is peacefully sleeping," we whisper, out of hearts of gentle kindness, to loved ones as we pass by lifeless shells. We do not want to face the cruel reality that who was once there...is gone. Change has occurred. Life will not be what it once was. The harsh reality of life is its temporality.

James understood the brevity of life.

> *"Come now, you who say, 'Today or tomorrow we will go to such and such a city, spend a year there, buy and sell, and make a profit'; whereas you do not know what will happen tomorrow. For what is your life? It is even a vapor that appears a short time and then vanishes away"* (James 4:13-14, NKJV).

A vapor that once filled the room suddenly evaporates and is gone. No wonder we often describe our emotion during grief as feeling empty. The rooms of our home are filled with empty. There is an empty spot on the sofa. The empty silence in the family laughter echoes the voice of the one who is not there. There is an empty place at the table. Next to mom is an empty place on the pew at church even though someone is sitting right next to her. Her bed is now half empty. In the middle of grief, the presence of empty is everywhere.

The reality of grief does not solely rest in death but in all the losses we experience in our lives. Loss comes from any number of sources including our own sin. Yet, we are reluctant to be transparent and genuine and grieve even our own sin because we know that what could have been…has been altered. Our grief however is never more real than when those we love pass from the temporal to the eternal.

Paul spoke of the reality of the view from grief's window as he wrote to the struggling church in Corinth, *"For we know that if our earthly house, this tent, is destroyed, we have a building from God, a house not made with hands eternal in the heaven. For in this we groan, earnestly desiring to be clothed with our habitation which is from heaven, if indeed, having been clothed, we shall not be found naked. For we who are in the tent groan…"* (2 Corinthians 5:1-4a, NKJV).

The Scriptures are not silent but murmur words of sorrow, mourning, suffering, pain, weeping, brokenness, and groaning. On more than one occasion God Incarnate, Jesus, wept because of the grief we carry in this life. At some point in life, we all fail to escape the icy tentacles of loss and the grief that follows. Death's cold fingers will one day encircle everyone we love, including us. All of us will pass through "the valley of the shadow of death." The road of life is less than smooth and to pretend that we will escape loss and grief is an exercise in futility.

As a young missionary, I learned a valuable lesson. The boarding school for the children of missionaries, where my wife and I served, hired an African gentleman to wash clothes for the 20 boys who were under our care. One morning as he arrived for work, he asked if he could get off early. When I inquired why, he told me that their baby had died during the night. My heart sank.

We had been married about 5 years at the time and we did not have any children and I could not comprehend on that sultry West African morning what it would be like to have a child and then see it die. I expressed my deep sorrow.

His response hit me like a load of bricks. "Well it is better that the baby dies now" he said, "They are cheaper to bury." I moved from deep sorrow to anger. How could he say that? In my self-assigned righteousness, I lectured him. He finally stopped me and spoke.

His words still echo. "Monsieur," he said in French, "you must remember, you are in Africa now and here death is part of life. Yes, I am sad and grieve but life must continue. I have other children and I must care for them. Am I sad? Oh sure I am sad. But death comes to everyone's house." I didn't want to think about the reality. That morning I walked past grief's window and glanced. It wasn't real however until I stood at its edge and gazed through the window of grief in my house. The pain is real. The sorrow is real. The emptiness is real. The emotions are real. Around that hospital bed I too faced the reality of the view from grief's window. The reality of the view is painfully normal.

It is not just in death that we experience the reality of grief. It comes when there is any sort of loss. A number of years after we left our ministry in Cote d'Ivoire a student asked if she could interview me for a missions class project. I agreed and the interview went well as we chatted about our sojourn in Africa and our ministry. It all went well until her last question. "What were you thinking the night before you left?" Seriously, how was I supposed to remember my thoughts from 15 years ago. The trouble was I remember very clearly what I thought. "I wish tomorrow would never come." Grief came flooding over me. This time I stood at grief's window and looked out at an uncertain landscape.

— **Chapter 2** —

The View Is Incongruent

The view from grief's window often does not make sense.
Sometimes grief can be confusing.

What do you do with the dissonance that is created by joy of one who is with the Father and the pain of separation? How do you make sense of the joyful memories of the past and the painful reality that the past is gone? How do you sort through emotions that seem rather incongruent? It is an emotional paradox…feeling two very different and even opposite emotions at the same time. You feel the pain of the loss and the delight in the suffering that has ended and the rest they have finally found.

Dad was 93 years old. His body was weak. His once strong gait had become a slow shuffle. Physically he had more bad days than good. He had committed his life to Christ. He was ready and in many ways, eager to pass from this life to the next.

His only hesitation was leaving mom. Even though she was still young and the stronger one, she was only 88. They had spent over 70 years together. The thoughts of being separated from her were not pleasant. One day sitting in the back yard, he said, "I wish me and mom could just lie down and go together." I reminded him that it didn't work that way. He just looked off into the distance…deep in thought. I knew. We all knew it was time for him to go. We wanted him to be free from the pain that now shared every day with him. And now he is free. We wanted his eyes to be clear again. And now they are.

But now when I return to Slocum and I walk into that little house, he is not there for me to kiss. His voice is silent when I want to ask him something. There are only memories of the lessons he taught us by living life in the simple lane. I can now see the hollow in mom's eyes and the quiver in her voice as she talks about her sweetheart. He's not there to give her his morning kiss. His place at the table is empty and he's not there to fry him sausage (with sage). I once told him eating that fried sausage would kill him one day. He would laugh and say, "Yeah probably." It did when he was 93. His laughter is only a memory now.

During every season, but winter, we spent hours sitting in lawn chairs in the backyard (mom and dad never had air conditioning and saw no need for it.). We would follow the shade of the big sycamore tree as the sun moved across the southern Ohio sky, and for hours he would talk of life and the most wonderful stories. When I was a little boy, a friend who had played minor league baseball, "Homebrew" Kline, would often join us and we would sit and listen to tales of playing ball. It felt like we were there at those bygone ballgames with them. But both their voices are silent now.

Dad's chair is still leaning up against the back of the house. One day shortly after his death, we all gathered again in the back yard.

When I got to the backyard all the chairs were taken except for dad's chair. In my mind, I knew I had not lived long enough to sit in that chair. I sat on the back steps.

So, what do you do with such incongruous emotions? It doesn't seem like they should be able to occupy the same place. How can we be joyful and sad at the same time? We tend to engage in a battle to let one of them go. If we cherish and hold too tightly to the memories, it seems like we deny the reality of the present. If we focus on the present, the pain can be overwhelmingly intense. Most of us are confident that the one who is gone would not want us to be sorrowful…but we are.

If you are fighting the battle and are weary and tired the solution is simple…surrender. Waive your white flag and declare an end to the war. The battle is over. The good news is neither wins nor loses. Solomon said it well, "There is a time to laugh and a time to cry." What am I suggesting? It's simple…fully embrace both emotions. Both emotions will be there. You can't escape them so put your arms around them and hold them. Both emotions are normal and it is okay to have them both. Quit fighting. You will have days when all you can think about are stories your loved one told and you will retell them. Or you will tell friends or family something they did that made your life what it is today. If you are around me very long I will tell you stories that dad told. My brothers and I now tell stories of Slocum and the steel mill. Our family shares ancient tales that were told of football, basketball, and baseball games we never attended.

There will be other days that you will be angry. They are not there when you need to ask them a question. You know if dad was here, he could tell you how to fix that lawn mower or what to do with your teenager. Mom could tell you how much salt you need in that recipe. As absurd as it sounds, it won't seem fair that they had to leave before they could tell you everything. As if they could tell you everything! Try writing down your anger. Just say, "I am angry and here's the reason why." In those moments, I don't think we are angry with the one who is not there nor are we angry with God. We are just angry at the temporality of life.

On other days, you will sit down and look at a faded photograph and cry. You will look at the calendar and remember that it is their birthday and will sorrow again. There will even be times that come unexpectedly when the pain will surge over you. You might be driving down the road and all at once you will start crying because you saw a tree or a cow or whatever and it will trigger a story and tears. Cry. If you have to pull the car on the side of the road for a few minutes, find a safe place and stop and cry.

You might be eating a meal and again the floodgate will open and no one will understand because they won't remember that he loved beans cooked that way or the bread plate will be sitting beside his place at the table. As the family gathers around the Thanksgiving table and the prayer is said and you look up and see again there is one missing and you will have to leave the room to cry. I say go ahead. Embrace all of those emotions. Don't try to defeat them. Just accept them.

I heard of a pastor who had gone to visit a nursing home on Thanksgiving. Sitting around the table were a group of elderly men and women eating a wonderful meal with turkey and all the trimmings prepared by the staff. The pastor noticed one dear elderly lady crying so he went over to talk to her.

"What's wrong," the pastor asked wanting to be a solace. He was sure she missed her children. Maybe it was her husband, he thought as he placed his gentle arm around her shoulder. "How can I pray for you," he whispered to her. "I miss my daddy," she said. He put his arm around the elderly lady, drew her fragile body close to him, and said "That must be very hard for you." He held his new friend and prayed in a quiet voice that only the two of them could hear and the God of all comfort. And he simply let her cry.

John tells the beautifully poignant story of a family who lost their brother.

> *So, when Martha heard that Jesus was coming, she went and met him, but Mary remained seated in the house. Martha said to Jesus, "Lord, if you had been here, my brother would not have died. But even now I know that whatever you ask from God, God will give you." Jesus said to her, "Your brother will rise again." Martha said to him, "I know that he will rise again in the resurrection on the last day." Jesus said to her, "I am the resurrection and the life. Whoever believes in me, though he dies, yet shall he live, and everyone who lives and believes in me shall never die. Do you believe this?" She said to him, "Yes, Lord; I believe that you are the Christ, the Son of God, who is coming into the world." When she had said this, she went and called her sister Mary, saying in private, "The Teacher is here and is calling for you." And when she heard it, she rose quickly and went to him. Now Jesus had not yet come into the village, but was still in the place where Martha had met him. When the Jews who were with her in the house, consoling her, saw Mary rise quickly and go out, they followed her, supposing that she was going to the tomb to weep there. Now when Mary came to where Jesus was and saw him, she fell at his feet, saying to him, "Lord, if you had been here, my brother would not have died." When Jesus saw her weeping, and the Jews who had come with her also weeping, he was deeply moved in his spirit and greatly troubled* (John 11:20-33, ESV).

I am confident Jesus' reaction to Mary and Martha did not make sense. He could have prevented this but He chose not to. He could have been there sooner but He chose not to. It simply did not make sense. The view from grief's window does not always make sense. It is incongruent. If your emotions do not always make sense, simply embrace each scene you see as you sit and stare out from grief's window.

— **Chapter 3** —

The View Takes
Us by Surprise

*The view from grief's window
very often takes us by surprise.*

My first view from grief's window took me by surprise. I am rather impulsive and laid back but I still don't like surprises, especially if they are negative. I don't like to get an unexpected bill. On the bills I am expecting, I don't want to find surprise charges that I knew nothing about. I don't even like surprise parties and I really don't like them if they are for me.

The door that leads to grief's window is nearly always jerked open suddenly even when we see God's hand on the door. While we may expect the door to be flung open, we don't expect it that week, or even that moment. The door was suddenly opened for me and there I stood in surprise at grief's window. I thought I was ready for my dad's death. For many years, I had thought about it. I had talked about it. Yet, the grief still took me by surprise. It was still an unexpected loss on that day and at that moment.

There are some deaths that do indeed take us by total surprise. An accident. A stillborn baby. A suicide. Illness that comes long before it should. While those do take us by surprise, the ones that aren't supposed to catch us off guard…do. I must admit that truth ambushed me. I wasn't expecting it.

Dad's death was not a surprise in the traditional sense. We knew Dad would soon step across the threshold that separates life from death. He was 93 and the laws of life and death would strongly suggest that he would soon be gone. Even when I was called away from a convention in Florida to come home, I knew it very well might be the last days I would spend with my dad.

On the airplane, I prayed as earnestly as I knew how that I would get to see my dad before he died. Even as a family friend graciously drove two hours to pick me up and we talked, I prayed. My prayer was not that he might not die but that he would live long enough for me to tell him I loved him one more time. Yet, I tried to prepare myself for a different outcome.

For more than 20 years I was anticipating dad's death. His parents died when they were in their twenties from tuberculosis. Dad always said that he would not live past 45. The Scripture says,

> *The days of our lives are seventy years; And if by reason of strength they are eighty years, Yet their boast is only labor and sorrow; For it is soon cut off, and we fly away* (Psalm 90:10, NKJV).

Dad was well into the bonus round. I thought I was expecting it. I thought I would be ready and there would be no surprises.

I have lived in other states and even overseas so for over 30 years and after high school had never been there to be with dad except for four or five visits a year. When dad became ill, my family had spent long hours at the hospital sitting with him. They all tried to meet every need they could without calling the medical staff. One of the family members was always in the room with him. When I arrived from the convention in Florida, I told them I wanted to stay with dad that night. And so, I sat up with him all night. I listened to the whispers of machines and quiet voices of the nursing staff. I sat in the corner at the foot of the bed. All night I kept a vigil on my little old daddy curled up in a hospital bed. I watched him breathe. I thought of some of the backyard stories and wondered if we could ever sit there again together. It was a wonderful night to be alone with my hero.

The next night I wanted to stay again, but my brother said he had gotten a good night's rest and insisted I get some rest while he stayed. I reluctantly agreed, but assured everyone that I would stay with dad the following night. I was looking forward to another night alone with him. However, to my surprise and deep sorrow the next night never came. He was gone by 1:00 PM the next day.

Mom was nearly 99 when I got the call I had expected for a long time. I just wasn't expecting it that day…at that time. I had just sat down to watch my beloved Buckeyes football game. My phone rang and I saw the caller ID, my sister-in-law. Something in the back of my mind knew, I knew what she was about to say. Mom had been slowly fading away for several years. She was in a nursing home being well taken care of, but her tired body was beginning to lose life's battle. My brother had been with her the day before and watched as she played "balloon volleyball" with some of the other residents. It was not Olympic caliber, but it did get these residents weary old arms to move a bit as they hit the balloon back and forth. She seemed fine.

The next day she had gone for lunch and then asked to be wheeled back to her room. When the staff went back to check on her a little later she was gone. I thought I would at least get to visit her one more time. The last few times I visited, she only answered when asked a direct question. Her mind was ebbing away and the Father chose to call her home that day. Shock, no...but there was still this element of surprise that this was that day.

We most often mark our lives by gains. How much we have earned. What we have accomplished or achieved. Most of us expect to achieve, to gain, to earn, and to have life turn out positively. It is little wonder that when loss comes it catches us by surprise. Just as we rejoice in life gains, we sorrow over losses. We are all aware that one of life's greatest losses is when death wraps its arms around those we love and we have to say goodbye. No one likes to say goodbye. A number of years ago a missionary's daughter said to me, "Heaven will be where we will never have to say goodbye. I am so tired of saying goodbye."

I wonder if Mary followed her son through Jerusalem's streets as He carried the cross on the shredded flesh of His back. Did she catch glimpses from grief's window or was she merely caught in the an- guish of the moment? As she stood on Golgotha's hill and watch life flow from her Son's body, I wonder if her grief took her by surprise. I wonder what she thought as she watched the Redeemer hang on the altar of the cross. She must have known He would be the Lamb that would take away the sin of the world. She must have known that the only sacrifice for sin was the shedding of blood...she must have known. I am sure she had thought for 33 years how it would hap- pen...but not this way...not this moment. Even though she knew it was inevitable, I wonder if it took her by surprise on that day. I won- der if the brutality and mockery caught her off guard. We have no way of knowing for the Scriptures are silent as to Mary's emotions. We know she was there and we know she loved her Son.

I can only imagine what Mary must have felt. I do know my griefs have caught me by surprise at the very moment the door was flung open and I stood tearfully beside that hospital bed or an unexpected phone call. Even when I thought I was totally prepared, I was sure of it...until I stood quietly, sobbing and looking at the barren landscape of loss from grief's window.

— Chapter 4 —

The View Highlights What Really Matters in Life

The view from grief's window provides a
view of those things in life that really matter.

A missionary friend, in his eulogy to his dad, said, "To be honest I struggled about returning from the field to be with my dad. I didn't have peace about the decision because I knew I was leaving our co-workers shorthanded. At 3:00 a.m. on Friday before he died on Saturday, he waved to me and said 'Bye-bye, I love you!' and I realized right then and there that it was the right decision and it was worth all the effort and expense to hear those words." The words were simple yet profound. "I love you" The truth is simple; we desperately need the affirmation of our parents, especially our fathers.

As I stood in front of dad's casket with my wife, I told her all I ever wanted was for him to be proud of me. The last night I stayed with him in the hospital, I was very tired. I had been called away at the end of a very busy convention. I was looking forward to being with Dad. But, I was also looking forward to some rest and sleep. I spent that night with Dad. I thought to myself, "I can be with Dad and still get several hours of much needed sleep." I can sleep in a chair as well as a bed so I knew I could get some rest…I was awake… all night. Dad would ask me to move him (sometimes just a half an inch would do), rub his back and feet, scratch his head or give him another shave. (He always had this aversion to whiskers).

He would ask me to soak a little sponge on the end of a stick in some cold water and let him suck on it. It was the only way he could get a drink. I rubbed the sponge around his dry lips. My eyes were heavy, but I wanted to do everything I could for my dad. He had done so many things for me. My hero looked so weak and vulnerable. At one point in the wee hours of the morning, as I was rubbing his back, my hands had been sitting near the air conditioning vent on the north side of the room. My touch was cool against his hot back. It was in that moment Dad said the most impacting words he ever spoke to me, "Oh, that's a good boy, that's a real good boy."

Oh, I don't suppose those nine words will go down in the annals of great hero speeches, but to a son, I wouldn't trade them for anything. You see he identified two simple things…I was his son and I had done something really well. I didn't have to hit a homerun, score a touchdown or make the winning basket. I just had to rub his back in the middle of the night.

I have to be honest; I would have stayed up a hundred nights to hear those words. I would have walked from Florida to have those words echo in my mind. Not one day has passed since I heard those words that I have not thought about them. As I stood in front of the casket with my wife, I realized that death emphasized what little time we have to give attention to the things in life that really matter.

Whether good or bad, we spend much of our lives of trying to accomplish something that has meaning and to hear someone say we have done it well. Even those who seem to follow the "beat of their own drum" are seeking the same thing. We all want affirmation for that which we do. We all want to believe that our lives matter and we have done something significant.

One wintry afternoon, I visited a dear saint in the hospital. Her tired body was curled under the blankets. Everyone seemed to know that her days were very short and soon she would transition from the temporal to the eternal. Her pastor was there. He turned to me and said, "You know, she is a real prayer warrior I count on her." I glanced her way and her eyes sparkled as her pastor explained. "Our church has a visitation program and this dear little lady and another elderly lady would love to go but physically they just aren't able to get around. So they stay and pray for our teams while we are out visiting." She never said much that day in the hospital except asking the pastor about various people who had been to the church as a result of their visitation…and their prayers. She was a warrior.

Jaimie, a missionary friend of mine, opened his remarks at his father's funeral by telling a humorous story of a young boy having a motorcycle accident and just before passing out someone asked him who he was and he said, "I'm Buddy Lancaster's boy. Today let me say I am proud to be Buddy Lancaster's boy." Jaimie then went for a long time telling why he was proud.

At 16 years old, dad left Slocum Station, Ohio, to find work in the Western forests. After one year, he made his way back to Slocum and vowed that if he ever got back he would never leave again. He kept that vow and except for very short visits to my brother's house in Indiana, he never left Slocum Station. Yet his impact has been profound, as evidenced by the hundreds of people who came by the funeral home to say goodbye to a little 93-year-old man. Who you really are, determines what you do. That dear old saint in the hospital, my friend's father, and my dad did the right things because they were the right kind of people.

The wallpaper on my computer screen is a scanned old black and white photograph of my dad and me. I am probably about 4 years old. I remember when mom took the picture. Dad was leaving for work. He was wearing his suede jacket. I can still smell it. Mom looked through her old Brownie Hawkeye and snapped the photo. The picture will never hang in a museum as a great work of art but it is my favorite photo of all time. It wasn't me doing something with dad. We were just together. My arms were wrapped around the man I admired so very much for who he was. I scanned the picture into my computer shortly after dad died. As I looked through grief's window, I wondered what photo my daughter would say is her favorite. Grief's window puts life into a new perspective.

When dad died, I remember those stories and that picture and it helped put life into perspective for me. I needed to focus far more on who I was than what I did. My character would lead to right actions. We will all make mistakes and err in our judgment but if we have Godly character those mistakes and errors will be less frequent and generally less intense.

There is also the life perspective grief's window brought to focus. As we lose one more of the old ones it means I am a little closer to being one of the old ones. There are not choices in life about aging. We can do all we can to hide it, cover it up, deny it but we are all getting older. In just a whisper of time, if it hasn't already arrived, we will be one of the old ones that the younger ones talk about. The question is, what will they see? What will they say?

How to ensure that the perspective on life the ones we leave behind is a far broader topic than this chapter or book can address. Just this simple statement, Godly character does not happen serendipitously it must be intentional.

We need to live. I don't mean to be alive but to really live. We need to live and encourage others to live. I need to affirm my wife, my daughter, my son-in-law, my grandson, my friends, and everyone else whose lives intersect with mine. I need to be kinder and gentler. I need to be more pleasant and less surly. I wonder what little things people do every day that I never say, "good job." I am always ready to point out when they don't live up to my expectations. When we wake up in the morning maybe we should ask ourselves, "Who needs a cool hand on their hot back in the middle of the night." My guess is far more people need a cool hand than a sharp tongue.

In those final years of mom's life, mom changed. She became quieter. She never was loud or even talked incessantly, but she was an encourager. Not just by her words but by her actions. My brothers were athletes and I don't suppose she ever missed a game. One thing you could always count on, mom was in the crowd. When, my wife and I answered the call to be missionaries in Africa, she was concerned (okay worried) but she never said, "Don't go." She stood with us and was proud. You could see it in her eyes. When I spoke in churches and she was there, I could sense her pride. She would often say, "You did a good job." Again, not profound words but ones that found a deep lodging place in the heart of one who struggled with feelings of inadequacy and insignificance. It was the substance of what really mattered.

When Jesus was a young twelve-year-old boy, His family made their annual trip to Jerusalem for the Feast of the Passover. When the feast was over Mary and Joseph were on their way home and noticed Jesus was not with them. I can almost hear the conversation,

"I thought He was with you."

"Well, I assumed He was with you"

"You shouldn't make assumptions!"

"I'm sorry, I just thought He would be with you…He always is."

"Where did you see Him last?"

"We better go back and see if we can find Him."

"I hope He's okay, He's probably scared." But you know the story, when they returned to Jerusalem they found Him in the temple. The elders were amazed at this child's command of the Scriptures and His knowledge. I wish I could have seen Mary's face. The worry lines no doubt had smoothed into the smile of pride. Don't you suppose when He looked into the crowd and saw His mom and dad grinning from ear to ear, He knew they were proud.

All of us, who are true followers of the Lamb, have spent our lives to hear our eternal Father say, "Well done." You know, I think maybe…just maybe…He will say to me…"That's a good boy… that's a real good boy."

— **Chapter 5** —

The View Is Different for Everyone

***The view from grief's window is never
the same for any two people.***

Bookstores have any number of books on their shelves dealing with grief. *Ten Steps to Find Peace after Loss, Wailing 101, Four Ways to Cope with Death,* etc.—and now this book! While there may be some value in them, I find the "cookbook" approach to grief problematic. I am not convinced that there is a proper way to grieve. Can I grieve one way and someone else grieve another way? My simple answer is yes. Every person experiences grief in a different way. Culture plays a significant role in our grieving process. It ranges from a stoicism to highly emotional. However, the demonstration of grief goes beyond cultural boundaries and is experienced differently among individuals in any particular culture. Some people will weep almost uncontrollably while others are silent. Some avoid people and want to be alone while others gather everyone they can around them. Just as individual personalities exist so does the way in which we grieve. Kubler-Ross has provided us with a nice and relatively neat outline of the "proper" stages of grief (Denial, Anger, Bargaining, and Acceptance). But this is simply a model. I wish it were so simple. Grief is messy. We can't wrap it up in paper and tie a nice bow around it. Grief is often ugly, complicated, and rarely the same for two people.

As we gathered around dad's bed in that hospital room, we knew he was dying, there was no denial. I even told one of my brothers that dad would not leave the hospital. Mom was nearly 99 years old and had been declining steadily physically and mentally for a number of years. I never felt the slightest tinge of anger. Instead they had lived very long and full lives. I never tried to bargain with God. Even if I could have the option of bringing them back, I wouldn't. All of our family simply accepted the fact that mom and dad were gone and for the next several days we simply allowed ourselves to weep at our loss, laugh at memories, and thank the Father for a wonderful gift He gave us in our parents. I remember as I tried to form the words of my wee prayer as we held hands around Dad's bed, I could only speak words of thanksgiving. I even prayed that the Father would graciously take mom on home. In the words of James Weldon Johnson, "She's labored long in my vineyard and she's tired and she's weary. Go down Death and bring her to me." It was time.

Several years ago, I went to a funeral home after a friend had died unexpectedly. My friend was in his 50s and left a wife and four children, two boys and two girls. The children were young adults. I watched with interest how each member of the family grieved. His wife was numbed. While she wept softly, I knew her grief would come later. The view from grief's window now was obscure and she could only see the shadows. One of the daughters stood near the rear of the funeral home and from the time I entered the room until

I left several hours later there was a constant river of tears etching its line down her cheeks. It was apparent that her relationship with her daddy was deep and so was her grief. The view from her window was very clear and she could see the stark realities of him being gone. She knew that the moments they shared were precious and were indelibly written on the tablets of her memory. She could not imagine life without him. Two of the children faced their father's death by denial. The denial looked very different, however. The son for the most part was absent. He would slip into the funeral momentarily and then leave as quickly as he came. The other daughter "worked" the crowd. She had the appearance of one grieving but her tears almost seemed plastic. She could cut them on and off at a moment's notice. It was as if they walked into grief's room but refused to even take a glimpse out of the window. The last son stood in relative silence near the casket. He cried very little. Every few minutes, he would turn and look at the lifeless body of his dad as if he wanted to say something. He would touch his hand and I could see him whisper something. His view was very much like his sisters', but rather than weeping he remembered. The point is simply that all five family members faced grief very differently.

I think the important issue is not **how** we grieve but that we allow ourselves **to** grieve. I have known those who felt as if they had to be stoic and not grieve. I have heard them say, "He/she wouldn't want me to be sad." The result is generally that they are always a wee bit sad for a very long time. It is as if they have chosen not to live. They often become bitter and even angry because they have not given release to their grief.

Grief does not mean we need to stop living. The day after dad's funeral, I had to leave to return to my home two states away. I called mom and asked her what she was doing and she said, "I'm canning green beans." I thought to myself, seriously, the day after we laid to rest your husband of 71 years and you are canning beans! "They are ready and dad would want us to go ahead and can them," she said. I could see them sitting in the back yard under that old sycamore tree stringing and snapping beans and talking about the little old man we all loved so much. I wish someone had taped the conversation. You see, life did not stop, it kept moving forward. By the way, I think Mom's "green bean therapy" was perfect.

The story is told of a minister who said, "One day they will put you in the ground and go back to the church and eat potato salad." The point is, life simply goes on. I am not trying to be morbid or uncaring, it is simply reality. We live and we die. I often think of the line from the movie Braveheart; William Wallace in his dying breath declared, "All men die but not all men truly live." Even after a loved one dies, we must continue to live.

The husband of my friend Mary passed away when he was in his 50s. He was a vibrant, enjoy life sort of guy. It was a tragic loss for Mary. But for some reason she remained very stoic and at least from anything I could gather she never allowed herself to grieve. The result was she had an "air" of sadness hovering over her the rest of her life. She was alive but had quit living. Life moves forward. It never is in reverse. So, allow yourself to grieve in whatever form that takes for you, but grieve.

When Jesus, after a few days' delay, showed up in Bethany, he did not rebuke Mary and Martha for their grief. John 11:35 notes that, "Jesus wept," as he stood outside Lazarus' tomb. While we may argue that grief was not the primary reason for his tears, I would suggest that at least in part he identified with Mary and Martha and shared in their sorrow.

There is not a fixed time limit on grief. I have heard people callously say, "He or she should be over it by now." I am not convinced there is a time frame assigned to our grief as long as we remember to live. The immediate pain of loss may lessen over time, but there is still loss.

— **Chapter 6** —

The View From Grief's Window Presents a New Perspective on Life

The view from grief's window refines our perspective on life...our worldview.

Our worldview basically answers three questions (although there are any number of variations): 1. Where did we come from? 2. Why are we here? 3. Where are we going? For the Christian, the first and third questions are relatively easy to answer, even though there are a multiplicity of views on where we come from. The view from grief's window brings into focus the real meaning or understanding of why we are here and what is our purpose.

Mom was a stay at home mom. It was a vocation she took as seriously as a corporate executive. Our house was small...no, it was tiny. Yet she managed to find enough to do that kept her busy all day...every day. Of course, when you had to draw water from the well to fill the ringer washer and hang the laundry on the lines stretched from the sycamore tree to the coal shed, I suppose you stay busy. When you raise, pick, and can nearly all of the vegetables for the long gray winter months, I suppose you stay busy. Not to mention, the hundreds of miles logged to ball games and practices of her boys. When she did sit down, she usually had a skein of yarn in her lap crocheting booties to keep in a shoe box so when a family friend had a new baby she would have gifts ready. The years took their toll on her body and she needed a hip replacement, but she refused to have it done. I've got to be here to "take care of Dad." It was her job…even though others could have helped and would be glad to "take care of dad," but it was her job and she wasn't going to relinquish it.

Soon after Dad passed away she agreed to have the surgery. My brother, Frank (always the responsible one) and his sweet wife Corina, took Mom to their home to recover. She never did quite recover from the operation. She developed drop foot and had trouble managing the simple movements of life. She was never able to return to that wee house on Lang-Slocum Road. The tiny little house that had been the center of our family was now sadly quiet and empty. For the next nine years, Frank and Corina CARED for mom. The change of perspective is so very obvious, the consummate caregiver now had to be taken care of.

My brothers and their wives cared for mom in ways that would leave our culture in slack-jawed amazement. Becoming caregivers instead of receivers transforms perspective. My oldest brother Blaine, said "I will do anything for mom after all she has done for us." Frank and Corina took mom into their home and made sure she had good home-cooked meals, took her medication, and accompanied her to doctor's appointments. They are a model of what it means to love deeply and to live sacrificial lives. Our family owes a huge debt to Frank and Corina.

My brother Mike and his wife Tami live just a few miles away. Mike worked full-time but most Saturdays would come and get Mom and take her to his house for the day. But that was after they made their stop at the local McDonald's. Their order was always the same. A fish sandwich, small fries, and a cup of coffee (with cream). They would drive to just up the road to the cemetery where Dad was buried. The cemetery sits on a hill with a panoramic view of the hills of Kentucky just across Ohio River, which winds its way through our community. They would sit in the car and eat their fish sandwiches and talk about life and especially about the "old" days. I'm sure Mike's perspective on life changed from those chats. Once their lunch was finished, they would go back to Mike and Tami's house to be doted on and fed another meal. He was cooking for her now.

For a couple of months each summer my oldest brother Blaine and his wife Beverly took Mom to their home in northern Indiana. Their house was always hub of activity. Blaine and Bev have five children, who have children, who have children so there was always a buzz of people coming and going. Even though she couldn't do much, Mom was able to enjoy the beehive of grandchildren and great grandchildren. She even had the chance to hold some great-great grandchildren.

And what about me and my wife, well I do carry a measure of guilt because I was not able to care for Mom like my brothers did. My work requires frequent travel and my wife Sheila was a nurse and worked 12 hours shifts. So, our house was empty much of the time and we didn't want Mom to sit alone all that time. But, even though my brothers seemed to understand, I felt and still feel significant guilt for not being able to help more. I visited as often as I could and a few times was able to go spend a week with Mom in order for Frank and Corina to get away for a few days. So, all of our perspective changed too in various ways. But one thing was for sure, we loved Mom and owed so very much to the woman who simply thought it was her responsibility to take care of us and her little house.

I've always been a dreamer about the future. Over the years, my dreams have changed, but many of my dreams have actually come true. I dreamed of being married and having a family. Check. I dreamed of living and serving overseas. Check. I dreamed of learning to speak another language. Check. I dreamed of being a doctor. Check (well sort of, I really wanted to be a physician but ended up being a psychologist, but a doctor nonetheless). Not everyone has those same dreams. What if the dream was to marry my high school sweetheart (I didn't have one but if I did…)? What if my dream was to get a good job and provide for my wife and family? What if my dream was to simply stay in my hometown be a good church and community member? The question is which dreams are more noble or of greater value.

I remember being at dad and mom's funerals and asking myself that question. Their dreams were not like mine at all. They had lived through two world wars and the Great Depression. Their dreams looked far simpler than mine. They led very quiet lives. Their dreams were indeed simple…for dad it was to have a good job and provide for his family. He worked in a steel mill (swing shift) for forty-five years, raised an enormous garden to feed us and several others who shared the bounty. For mom, it was to nurture and care for her husband and her boys…that's all. Years after his death, I learned something about my dad and mom I never knew, how several families would not have had Christmas had my dad and mom not provided for them. They did it quietly with no public mention or fanfare. Even though they died in their 90s the funeral home was packed with those whose lives were touched by the simple and quiet lives of my parents.

I guess we can argue which is more valuable, a quarterback or the line who protects him. A dead-eye shooter in basketball or the point guard who makes sure he has the ball at the right time. Whose lives were more valuable in the Kingdom, Paul's or the folks at the church at Philippi whom he loved and who apparently were faithful in the ministry to Paul and the church? Whose lives were more noble in Hebrews 11, those whom God delivered or performed miracles or the "and others" who were tortured, beaten, and killed?

I'm afraid far too often I place more worth or value on the "stars." Ashamedly, I fail to give kudos to those who live in the simple lane of life. They deserve far more than they receive. Yet, a large part of what makes these people so beautiful is they aren't looking for "atta boys." They simply live life, love those around them, and faithfully serve the Father.

I am often an "up-front" guy. I must remember I wouldn't be up-front unless there were people to be in front of. To be sure, the Father gives each of us roles to play in the Kingdom. If you live life in the simple lane…thank you. I appreciate so very much all you do. If you are an "up-fronter" be sure to say thanks sincerely and often to those who make your role possible.

When dad died, I remember those stories and that picture and it helped put life into perspective for me. I needed to focus far more on who I was than what I did. My character would lead to right actions. We will all make mistakes and err in our judgment, but if we have godly character those mistakes and errors will be less frequent and generally less intense.

Grief's window again brought the notion of lifespan into focus. Recently, I have come to the realization that most of my life is now in the rearview mirror. I am one of those strange people I suppose that would love to live life over again…even if I didn't know what I know now. I have enjoyed most of my life. It has been filled with joy and adventure. But, it is on a crash course for death and it seems to be picking up speed. I am not trying to be morbid…just honest.

For years, I was one of the "young ones," but not anymore. I even find myself reading more obituaries and wondering what will be said about my life.

When I have taken my last breath, life will continue to move forward. Life did not depend on me being here and will not halt when I have left. I am often sobered by the fact that I know nothing about my great grandparents and very little about my grandparents as they were all four gone before I was born. It reminds me that in a few short years after I am gone only a few may remember me or anything about me. Sobering.

The best example is not one of my stories but what Paul wrote in his letter to the church at Philippi,

> *Have this mind among yourselves, which is yours in Christ Jesus, who, though he was in the form of God, did not count equality with God a thing to be grasped, but emptied himself, by taking the form of a servant, being born in the likeness of men. And being found in human form, he humbled himself by becoming obedient to the point of death, even death on a cross* (Philippians 2:5-9, ESV).

Why was Jesus sent to earth? The answer is simple, to love the Father, to serve, and to die. We can ask the question, what did Christ empty Himself of? He emptied Himself of Himself to become a servant and to be obedient. My dad and mom emptied themselves to serve others and to be obedient to the Father.

The view from grief's window has certainly refined my world-view. I more clearly understand why I am here.

— Chapter 7 —

Once You Have Looked Through Grief's Window You Will Always Remember What You Saw

When I took my first look through grief's window I knew I would never be the same. I knew I would never look at life and death quite the same.

Every summer the mission agency where I work, sends over one hundred high school and college age students across the globe. During the first evening of training, the parents are still there and I nudge them to say goodbye and leave. Okay it is more than a nudge; I tell them to leave because we have things to do. I try to help them say goodbye to their student. They continue to want to hang around, so eventually I have to tell them it is time to leave. But I always instruct them to tell their children goodbye, because they will not get the same one back. My words are always, "They can't 'un-see' what they will have seen and they will never be the same."

When we experience significant loss, we are never quite the same. We may go back into our normal flow of life, but there is something that is not quite the same. The intensity of the change diminishes over time, but there will almost always be a change.

I would have loved to have talked to Mary, Martha, and Lazarus after Lazarus had been raised from the dead. I am quite confident their lives were significantly changed. There is little doubt they had a whole new perspective on life and death.

When I was in graduate school, one of the major papers we were required to write was our theory of change. That is, what are the underlying factors and principles that bring about change in people's lives. Since I was studying counseling psychology, I completely understood the assignment. By definition, what we were trying to learn to do was create an environment where our clients would change. They would not be seeing us if nothing needed to change. The pleasant or unpleasant truth is the ebb and flow of life changes us. We change as our bodies mature. Change occurs when we go off to school, leave home, get married, and have children. The same is true when those we love die. We are changed.

The disciples were ready to conquer the world and to establish the Kingdom of God when Jesus was with them. Then they found themselves in a room with their Messiah and He began to do and say some strange things. He washed their feet. He broke bread and gave them wine. He said, "*This is my body which is broken, this is my blood that is shed.*" Their minds must have reeled when He told them I'm going away and you can't come with me. What?! I often wonder what must have gone through their minds. They had left everything to follow Him and then He springs this news on them. Not many hours passed until He was hanging on the cross…dead. The next thing we hear about the disciples is that they are hiding in fear. His death changed them from men ready to conquer the world to men trembling in fear. (By the way, they were changed again by His resurrection, hallelujah!) But they would never forget what they saw.

For most of us, after the initial stages of our grief, most people would not be able to detect the change. We go about our daily lives, but tucked away, there is this emptiness. We can pull it up when we think about it. Even as I type these words, across my desk is a picture of my mom and dad. Each time I look at them there is a longing for what was. There is a yearning to sit again in the backyard following the shade of the Sycamore tree. I want to sit in those lawn chairs and listen to the stories all over again. We had a family friend, Homebrew Kline. (Not sure where he got his nickname, but I think I can figure it out!) He had been a professional baseball player and he and dad would sit for hours in our back yard and my brothers and me would listen to tales of baseball games from days long ago. It would be wonderful if I could sit on those back-porch steps and watch mom hang clothes on the lines that stretched from the sycamore tree to the coal shed. But I can't, they are gone now. So, when I see their picture, I think of the stories and scenes from the past, which I cannot relive except in my mind. The hollowness of their absence is palatable.

By the way, as you process grief, one of the important healing salves are the stories. Tell them, tell them as often as you need to tell them. When my family gets together there is always some story to tell of our parents. Their stories keep them "alive" in our hearts and memories. We've told them over and over. If the stories ignite bad memories use them as a springboard to forgiveness.

I often pause and ask myself what are the stories and scenes my daughter will see when she pictures my wife and me when we are gone. Will she long for days to relive those moments? I may be too nostalgic, but the old days carry a lot meaning for me. But do you know what they talked about in the good old days, yeah, they talked about the good old days. I remind myself often that these are someone's good old days and I want to do all I can to make them good because you can't un-see what you have seen.

Hebrews 11 gives us a catalogue of memories. Men and women who had been faithful. I think the writer of Hebrews understood the importance of remembering and helping us not un-see things that had been seen. Would you have loved to be sitting with the disciples following Jesus' ascension and listening to the stories of all they had seen? I am convinced they were able to process their grief by constantly keeping in their minds and on their lips the things they saw as they were mentored and ministered to through the life of our Lord. John even wrote,

> *This is the disciple who is bearing witness about these things, and who has written these things, and we know that his testimony is true. Now there are also many other things that Jesus did. Were every one of them to be written, I suppose that the world itself could not contain the books that would be written"* (John 21:24-25, ESV).

Maybe one day we will get to hear the stories of the "many other things that Jesus did." I can almost hear the disciples' voices as they moved about in their ministries following the ascension. Don't you know that Peter at some point said, "Andrew, do you remember the day you told me I had to meet this guy, the Messiah? We were both so moved that we dropped everything to follow Him. I am so embarrassed that after His death I went back to the things I left behind. I'll never do that again, Andrew...never."

Stories...tell them.

— **Chapter 8** —

Grief Is a Painful Process

***When we stand at grief's window the scene is
accompanied by an immeasurable amount of pain.***

Late in the summer of 1980, Sheila and I traveled back to Slocum Station, Ohio and the little gray shingled house that sat near the bottom of the hill. Nothing much had changed in the house other than natural aging of the house and the couple who made it a home. This trip was to say goodbye before my wife and I were to leave for language study in France, and then on to Ivory Coast, West Africa. They were not "old" then, but it seemed they were. I told them that if something were to happen to them I probably would not be able to return. I don't remember much of the weekend. I am sure mom cooked; the rest of the family visited. I am sure we went to church on Sunday and said our goodbyes there. Those memories are probably stored in some room of my brain, but I can't find the key to unlock the door. But maybe I can't remember because there is the one memory that is the most vivid and it simply drowns out the other memories. On Sunday afternoon, the moment came when we would have to get in our car and head back to our Tennessee home to finish the last-minute packing before setting off to France. Mom and dad walked us to the car. I wrapped my arms around them, told them I loved them. Tears filled our eyes. They were fearful they would never see their baby boy and his wife again. While that may seem a little overly dramatic, I am relatively confident that was what was racing through their minds. I can still see the look on their faces…PAIN.

We experience something very similar when we lose someone close…pain. It hurts. Even when we know it is for the better…it hurts. Dad was nearly 94 and mom was close to 99 when they crossed over Jordan's river. They had lived long and very healthy lives until the years finally caught up with them. Their bodies finally and simply wore out. We all knew it was time for them to go and at a certain level were very glad for the them to make the crossing…but it was still painful. It hurt. No matter how many times we have to say goodbye, and we do a lot during our lifetimes, it never gets easier, only more familiar.

The accomplished guitarist, Chet Atkins, wrote and sang a song about his dad. Atkins was well-known for his brilliant guitar mastery, but not his singing. If you hear him sing you know why. I wouldn't say he is a horrible vocalist but he certainly did not win a Grammy for vocal performance. But I find myself, regularly pulling this song up on YouTube and playing it. In his honest and humble voice, the song reminds me of the pain of loss. You can hear ache in his voice as he sings, "I Still Can't Say Goodbye." It isn't the sting of acute pain but an ache, a longing, a fond but sad remembrance.

We find ourselves echoing Paul's words to the church at Corinth. *"When the perishable puts on the imperishable, and the mortal puts on immortality, then shall come to pass the saying that is written: 'Death is swallowed up in victory.' 'O death, where is your victory? O death, where is your sting?' The sting of death is sin, and the power of sin is the law"* (1 Corinthians 15:54-56, ESV). For the believer there is still a sting…but the sting is overcome by victory.

Mom and dad were old. I was anticipating the sting. When my wife and I were in language school in France, we lived in an upstairs apartment of a French family. It was interesting in the early months trying to communicate. Marc and Simone treated us wonderfully. Marc was a beekeeper. Behind the house were about ten beehives. I would watch him go out to the hives with no protection. He would lift the lids and look inside. The bees acted as if they knew him and they no doubt did. One evening, after I learned enough French to have a very simple conversation, Marc said to me, "J'ai besoin ton service ce soir," (I need your help this evening). Two things struck me in that simple verbal exchange. One, I understood him and was able to respond…language progress. Two, it was a chance to repay the kindness Marc and Simone had shown to Sheila and me. I was glad until he told me what he needed my help for. He wanted me to help him move one of the hives. Yikes. I said, "Marc, I'm scared of bees." He told me we could wait until the evening when they were all in the hive and we could put something over the door. It still wasn't enough reassurance to allay my fears, but I was willing. The evening came and with trepidation I followed him to the hive we were to move. He placed a board over the entrance. When we picked the hive up you could hear them buzzing inside. Fortunately, they were all in for the evening…except one and he was NOT happy. I was anticipating the sting. It finally stung Marc, who seemed rather immune to the pain.

Not unlike that evening in France, as mom and dad grew older and feebler, I anticipated the sting. There were moments of anxiousness and dread even though I knew it was inevitable. I knew the immediate pain would be there. No matter how much courage I wanted to muster, how tough my hide might be, I knew the sting was coming...and it did and at moments it is still there. To be sure the acute pain is gone but the lingering sting remains.

— Chapter 9 —

The Darkest View

Sometimes you are suddenly thrust in front of grief's window unexpectedly and the darkness of the view is overwhelming.

Dad fell and broke his hip. It had to be repaired for him to have any semblance of normal life. My family arranged for the surgery and Dad was admitted to the hospital. The surgery went well, but soon his body began to retain fluid. Dad never came home. He was almost 94. He had lived a long life. I don't want to sound uncaring, disrespectful, or morbid, but it was time for him to go. I suppose we all knew that one day it would come. So, in one way, when it is inevitable it softens the grief at least for a moment. But what about the times you are suddenly thrust in front of grief's window unexpectedly.

I remember the first time I looked through the unexpected dark window.

The school year had just ended and my brothers and I were ready for the warm days of summer filled with fishing, playing ball, and spending more time in the woods. Just across the road and up a hill from our house lived our aunt and uncle. We all loved Uncle Bud and Aunt Corbia as much as any boys could possibly love someone. Aunt Corbia taught us about birds and wildflowers (I can still name most of them to this day). Uncle Bud was every boys dream uncle. He was in his 50s but never quite grew up. He was always full of fun. Uncle Bud bought the first TV in our neighborhood, but Aunt Corbia made him put it in the basement. They set up chairs for the neighbors to come watch this new-fangled contraption. He took us fishing and would sing a hundred goofy little songs, played ball with us, and taught our Sunday School class at church. One day, Uncle Bud took my brother and me fishing. We were going to a small river and on the way, we had to cross an old covered bridge. When we got to the bridge there was a sign that said 1 Ton Limit. Uncle abruptly stopped the car and said, "Neil you need to get out and walk across the bridge, I am afraid you might make us overweight." I doubt if I weighed 50 pounds. I don't remember another thing about the trip, but I remember the joy I had skipping across the bridge and thinking what wonderful adventures we had with our uncle. In our eyes, Uncle Bud was the best.

But this summer would be different. Uncle Bud was sick. One evening, he managed to feel well enough to come to the yard and play whiffle ball with us. He even fell over a doghouse trying to catch a fly ball and we all laughed including Uncle Bud. The next day, he went to the hospital. They thought he had some ulcers and they were going to treat him. They discovered something much worse. He had cancer. The doctors did surgery and the news was grim. A few short days later, Uncle Bud was gone. My brothers and I were devastated. The rest of the family was too. I was only eleven and didn't know how to handle the death of someone so close. I remember going to the funeral home, but I wouldn't go next to the casket. I slid to the back of the room. I couldn't wrap my mind around the truth that Uncle Bud was gone. He was in his 50s. It wasn't time yet, I thought to myself. The view was simply too painful for an eleven-year-old boy to navigate.

I wish that was the only time I looked out the darkest window of grief. But it isn't and I suppose there will always be times when those close to us will leave long before we think they should.

Some of you have experienced darker views than I can ever imagine. I have a daughter, her husband, and a grandson. I cannot begin to imagine how I would react if I lost any of them, but some of you have. You have stood in front of grief's darkest window. You gazed through the shaded panes with more pain than you thought you could endure. I've often thought about those who sent their sons and daughters off to war. You have seen the scenes in movies. A mom is going about her daily chores and looks out the kitchen window and sees two officers slowly walking to her door. Her heart sinks and her stomach is in a knot. She walks to the door trying to hold back her emotions because she knows why they are there.

My brother is two years older than me. His class had just graduated and one of his classmates and our close friend joined the Navy. He was home on leave. He came out to our house to show Dad a new shotgun he had purchased. The next day he was riding his motorcycle down a section of the highway that was flat and straight. Something happened. He lost control and crashed. His head hit the guard rail and he was instantly killed. I remember the shock and grief our family experienced. I don't remember the funeral at all. However, two things happened at the cemetery that left indelible imprints in my memory. The military gave our friend a 21-gun salute. The pop of the rifle hauntingly echoed across the hills of Southern Ohio. The second thing that I can see as clearly as if it was a few minutes ago was the look on the face of our friend's father. He had just taken a look out of grief's darkest window.

Since that time, I have walked with many of my friends who have found themselves in that very dark place. All of us at some point in life will try to offer words of comfort and care to those who are with broken hearts gazing across the hostile landscape. But the reality is there are no words…none. What do you say to a wife, son, and daughter who are burying a husband and dad who has died long before his allotted time? What words are there to offer to a parent who has watched their child slip into eternity…none. All we can do is be there, really there.

There is another dark grief that I often refer to as the "hidden grief." It happens more often than we might realize because many of those who find themselves looking out of this window, do it alone. They often don't share this alarming moment of life that is so devastating. A young couple discovers they are going to be parents. The excitement of having a new little one puts a smile on their face and heart. Then something happens, the mom notices that something is wrong. They journey to the nearest ER in panic. The dreams of holding a newborn, decorating a room, walking into church with the bundle of joy in their arms comes to a sudden halt as they hear the words…miscarriage. Anger. Questions. Guilt. Grief. Empty. Since, the baby has been "hidden" in the mother's womb they chose to grieve with only a few friends and family. Some of those who try to help, will crack the door and peek in at the one standing by the dark window. They will want to say something but the words stick to the roofs of their mouths. My hope is that they will open the door, walk to the one by the window, wrap their arms around them, and simply weep with them. Allow them to say what they want and listen.

The biblical account of a young mom standing at grief's darkest window always moves me.

> *Now the wife of one of the sons of the prophets cried to Elisha, "Your servant my husband is dead, and you know that your servant feared the Lord, but the creditor has come to take my two children to be his slaves." And Elisha said to her, "What shall I do for you? Tell me; what have you in the house?" And she said, "Your servant has nothing in the house except a jar of oil." Then he said, "Go outside, borrow vessels from all your neighbors, empty vessels and not too few. Then go in and shut the door behind yourself and your sons and pour into all these vessels. And when one is full, set it aside." So she went from him and shut the door behind herself and her sons. And as she poured they brought the vessels to her. When the vessels were full, she said to her son, "Bring me another vessel." And he said to her, "There is not another." Then the oil stopped flowing. She came and told the man of God, and he said, "Go, sell the oil and pay your debts, and you and your sons can live on the rest"* (2 Kings 4:1-7, ESV, emphasis mine).

So, a young mom has lost her husband. She's knee deep (maybe neck deep) in debt. Her sons are about to be taken from her and forced into slavery to pay off the debt, which seems a little harsh, but remember in the Old Testament they did not play around! She didn't know what to do so she made a beeline to the prophet. I can almost hear the painful anguish in her voice as literally everything that was important to her in life was about to be swept away from her. Her emptiness was about to become bigger than she thought she would be able to endure. I am confident there were tears etching lines down her face. Her voice had to be cracking as she tried to get her desperate message to the prophet. Maybe she had exhausted all her connections to find help first and ended up at Elisha's doorstep. Maybe Elisha's house was her first stop. Perhaps her boys were with her. I don't know but I *do* know this…she is about to lose it all and she was at the end of her rope and didn't seem to even know how to tie the proverbial knot to hang on.

The prophet asks her what seems to me to be a bit of a strange question. "What do you have at your house?" I think I would have said, "Well, sir, we have an old sofa we got at the Jerusalem Goodwill. It's not much, but it is ours. We have three old mattresses that someone gave us. There's a beat-up table and four chairs" and her voice cracks as she remembers that one of the chairs is now empty. Her husband was gone. "Sir, we just don't have much at all. The food is nearly gone and about all we have left is this little bottle of oil." I wonder if the old prophet looked off into the distance, smiled and said, "There's not enough *empty* at your house." Elisha said tell your boys to go find every can and bottle they can find from the neighbors…but make sure they are empty. Seriously Elisha, we need money…we need a loan…we need something we can sell…we don't need a bunch of emptiness there is plenty of that for the rest of my life. But she trusted the prophet, and she hustled the boys out the door and around the neighborhood. "Hurry boys, find as many vessels as you can. I don't know what he will do with them but Elisha says he needs them." Off they ran scampering from house to house, they didn't have time to tell the whole story but promised they would bring their pots and bottle back, but the prophet needed them. People were generous and soon the boys had all the vessels the neighbors could spare. There were vessels of every shape and size. They shut the door and the boys sat on the floor and watched in eager anticipation as their mom did what the prophet had asked her to do. He told the widow, take your little bottle of oil and pour it into a pot. She probably didn't understand why, but as she began to pour, the oil didn't stop and soon the pot was full. She was speechless. That little bottle of oil was too small to fill that pot...but it did. She said, "Boys bring another pot." I'm pretty confident they scrambled as fast as they could and watched with their mouths wide open as she filled pot after pot out of that little bottle? By the time they sat the last vessel in front of their mom, they were dancing with delight. "Boys bring me another one." "There isn't any more momma."

She ran to Elisha's house with the boys kicking up the dust as they ran. Elisha looked at the mom and winked at the boys and said, "Now go sell the oil and pay your debts and thank the Father."

Did you notice what the prophet said, "There is not enough empty"? I wonder if the beauty of the dark grief is that it empties us so we can be filled with Him. When our emptiness is filled with His unmistakable presence, there is a balm for our souls that no words can bring. May each of you who find yourselves staring out this ominous window find comfort in His sweet presence.

Chapter 10

A View of Hope

*We cannot escape the view from grief's window,
but for the Christ follower, we gaze with hope.*

Grief is indeed a reality. Reality is often harsh and painful. At times, grief creeps into our lives unexpectedly but we all will experience it. Grief, however, is different for the believer. Our grief wraps itself around the truth of hope. We find our comfort, as River Valley Worship declares, "Hope has a name, His name is Jesus." Because of the death, burial, and resurrection of Jesus, we have life, not just in this world, but throughout eternity. While in the moment, we grieve because what once was is no longer, but for the follower of Christ one day this temporal life will come to an end and we will cross Jordan's stormy banks and reach eternity.

For the first 23 years of my life, Dad was not a Christ follower. As I said in the prologue, every night Mom would kneel beside her bed and pray out loud. Our house was so tiny I could always hear what she prayed for. Her voice and heart carried all of us to the throne, including Dad and he would be in the bed. She never gave up and for nearly 50 years she prayed. I prayed for him too. I never told anyone, but while I was away at college, I would often spend the entire night praying for Dad. I would not be able to sleep for worrying about the man who was truly my hero. He was getting older and I didn't want him to enter eternity without giving his heart to Christ. I was home from the Bible college I was attending at the time. I had a wonderful supper of Mom's home cooking and good conversation all evening. I laid down for the night. From my bed once again, I listened to Mom pray. As I was about to doze off, I could hear Mom and Dad talking. I couldn't decipher what they were saying, so I rolled over for a night's rest in my old familiar bed. Suddenly Mom called for me, "Neil can you come in here, Dad wants to get saved." It was a wonderful moment as he repented of his sins and wonderfully gave his heart to Christ. Mom's prayers, along with many others prayers, were answered that night. Anxiety was replaced by hope.

I have always loved Isaiah 40 as the Lords comforts His people. The chapter ends with a very familiar refrain:

> *Have you not known? Have you not heard? The Lord is the everlasting God, the Creator of the ends of the earth. He does not faint or grow weary; his understanding is unsearchable. He gives power to the faint, and to him who has no might he increases strength. Even youths shall faint and be weary, and young men shall fall exhausted; but they who wait for the Lord shall renew their strength; they shall mount up with wings like eagles; they shall run and not be weary; they shall walk and not faint* (Isaiah 40:28-31, ESV).

Grief bring weariness, but for the Christ follower, He provides the hope of strength. Just when we think we can bear no more, He provides supernatural strength. Our weariness has turned to walking, walking in hope. And as if that isn't enough the prophet adds in chapter 43:

> *But now thus says the Lord, he who created you, O Jacob, he who formed you, O Israel: "Fear not, for I have redeemed you; I have called you by name, you are mine. When you pass through the waters, I will be with you; and through the rivers, they shall not overwhelm you; when you walk through fire you shall not be burned, and the flame shall not consume you (Isaiah 43:1-2, ESV).*

Not only does He provide strength. He promises us His presence. Even in the darkest moments of our lives He is there. When Mom and Dad died, I sensed His presence in a very real way. There was this sense of inner joy, for I know they had lived life well. I have always said they lived life in the simple lane. There was nothing extraordinary about their lives, just country folks who lived life well. When it was their time to cross into eternity, there was a sense of peace that only comes from the Father. It is the hope of knowing it was simply a transition from earthly to heavenly.

What did He give Mary and Martha? Hope. What did He give the centurion whose daughter was gone? Hope. What did He give the thief on the cross? Hope. What did He give to my family? Hope. Hope in what though? Hope in knowing this is not the end. Hope in the realization that our separation is only temporary. Hope in the peace that supersedes the storm. Hope in eternity together with our loved ones and people from every tongue, tribe, and nation. Hope in the reality that we will be with our Redeemer and Savior for ever and ever.

So yes, we grieve but as Jesus reminded us in the Sermon on the Mount:

> *Blessed are those who mourn, for they shall be comforted* (Matthew 5:4, ESV).

On two separate occasions Paul wrote words of encouragement to the church at Corinth.

> *For this light momentary affliction is preparing for us an eternal weight of glory beyond all comparison, as we look not to the things that are seen but to the things that are unseen. For the things that are seen are transient, but the things that are unseen are eternal* (2 Corinthians 4:17-18, ESV).

> *When the perishable puts on the imperishable, and the mortal puts on immortality, then shall come to pass the saying that is written: "Death is swallowed up in victory." "O death, where is your victory? O death, where is your sting?" The sting of death is sin, and the power of sin is the law. But thanks be to God, who gives us the victory through our Lord Jesus Christ. Therefore, my beloved brothers, be steadfast, immovable, always abounding in the work of the Lord, knowing that in the Lord your labor is not in vain* (1 Corinthians 15:54-58, ESV).

How can we forget John's poignant words in Revelation?

> *He will wipe away every tear from their eyes, and death shall be no more, neither shall there be mourning, nor crying, nor pain anymore, for the former things have passed away* (Revelation 21:4, ESV).

In John chapter 14, Jesus told His disciples He was going away to prepare a place for us, an eternal home with our Savior and Redeemer. So, for a Christ follower, we need not mourn as those with no hope. We have hope. Time does not stop. Our days are numbered. We say goodbye but not farewell.

Here is the reality of life, just around the bend in the road, our family and friends will gather some place to grieve our passing. Recently, my grandson reminded me of this harsh reality. He had a lot of "God" questions.

"Papa, mom said your mom and dad are dead and are in Heaven," he said with a 7-year-old serious tone.

"Yes, they are," I replied, not knowing where this was headed but wanting to answer his questions.

"What's it like there?"

"I don't know; I have never been."

"How old are you Papa?"

"Well, I'm 66."

"Oh, so you're almost dead too."

Well, that is not where I wanted the conversation to go, but he was right. One day my family and friends will sing a few songs, say some kind words (I hope), and life will move forward. Once again, they will stand at grief's window and look across the desolate landscape of separation. But when they peer in the distant they will see the light of hope. They will see the face of Jesus. The view from grief's window may be painful but it will not be the end. May He always find us faithful even in the midst of our grief.

Epilogue

When mom and dad died, I was 51 and 61. I had a Ph.D. in counseling psychology. I worked with numbers of people who were trying to make their way through the dark valley I had just entered. I knew the process grief follows and the techniques to use to help them on that journey. But the day dad died, it was mom who was the counselor and I, her client. Now, Mom was not one of those people who would sit you down to teach you something, she just demonstrated in the way she lived life in the simple lane. The day after we buried dad, my wife and daughter finished packing up our things. We had to leave mom sitting in the backyard stringing, snapping, and canning beans. Oh, from time to time she wept, after 71 years of marriage she should have and did, but she also knew that life continues and so must she. She couldn't dwell indefinitely in grief. Ten years later when mom died, I remembered her lesson. I didn't have beans to can, but I knew that it was okay to move forward in life, and it was okay to stop from time to time and weep.

Grieve...it's okay.

First Aid for
Your Emotional Hurts booklets

Depression
ISBN 13: 9780892656301

Grief
ISBN 13: 9780892656325

**First Aid For Your Health:
10 Therapeutic Life Changes**
ISBN 13: 9780892656837

Dr. Moody, author of *First Aid for Emotional Hurts*, is following up his successful book to pastors and laypeople seeking to reach out to help people with a series of booklets addressing specific issues people face. The booklets contain a biblical model for recovery and give appropriate resources for problems requiring professional help. The author also provides contact information for many sources providing help. Dr. Moody speaks with a qualified voice to the emotional, physical, and spiritual needs in various situations faced in today's society.

www.randallhouse.com

randall house
randallhouse.com

Available as an e-Book

Battling the Black Dog
Raw Confessions of Depression in Ministry

by Randy Sawyer
Paperback
ISBN 13: 9780892655205
$13.99

When leadership responsibilities are linked to warfare with the world, the flesh, and the devil, you have the formula for all kinds of stress disease and depression.

This book shares the personal experience of the author as he survived two bouts with depression and so much more. Physical, emotional, psychological, and spiritual symptoms of depression are addressed as well as common causes of depression. The author spends a good amount of time dealing with nine spiritual disciplines that become a significant part of reaching a cure for depression and hindering repeat bouts in the future. He speaks with the voice of experience and a strong desire to help those in ministry find a way to overcome the profound impact of depression on the individual, the family, and the ministry.

www.randallhouse.com

randall house
randallhouse.com

What is **D6**?

BASED ON DEUTERONOMY 6:4-7

A **conference** for your entire **team**

A **curriculum** for every age at **church**

An **experience** for every person in your **home**

Connecting
CHURCH & HOME
These must work together!

D6 CONFERENCE
ONCE A YEAR

DEFINE & REFINE Your Discipleship Plan

www.d6family.com

ONE HOUR
A WEEK

POWER OF
PARENTAL INFLUENCE

D6 Conference

a conversation. a platform. a gathering.

Bridging churches and homes
to the **heart of Deuteronomy 6.**

Connect with us online
D6conference.com